Learning to Cook for My Man

Romance through Food

101
Delicious
Recipes

FOR BEGINNERS

LaShona Patton-Jones

DEDICATION

This book is written and dedicated to my mother Mattie Williams Patton and to Dr. Gloria Scott. They both taught me a lot about food and how food has kept the family together. I am so happy to have written this book from the lessons I've learnt from you.

The recipes in this book speak love, harmony, wellness and family bond.

Thank you for reading.

LaShona Patton-Jones

1. HOT PEACH SALSA

Ingredients

- 2 (15-oz) cans peaches, drained and chopped, although If you want to make this California style—use fresh peaches.
- 2 green onions, sliced thin, including tops
- 2 tablespoons lime juice
- 2 teaspoons chopped fresh cilantro
- 2 teaspoons garlic chili sauce
- ¼ dash of cayenne pepper
- 1/2 teaspoon five spice powder
- 1/4 teaspoon white pepper

Procedure

1. In a bowl, mix the drained, chopped peaches, sliced green onions, chopped cilantro, garlic chili sauce, lime juice, five spice powder, white pepper.
2. Mix well.
3. Chill before serving.

2. CREAM CHEESE WONTON

Ingredients

- 1 cup cream cheese
- 16 wonton wrappers or 24 egg roll wrappers
- oil (for frying)
- a sweet and sour sauce

Procedure

1. Heat oil in a deep-fat fryer or pour into a deep skillet on high temperature. Vegetable oil or peanut oil works best.
2. While oil is heating, lay out as many wrappers as you plan to use. Have a small bowl of water nearby to wet your fingers. Put a small dab of cream cheese in one corner of each wrapper, about 1/2" from the edges. Use about 2 tsp. for egg roll wrappers or 1 tsp. for wonton wrappers. Using your fingers, wet the two edges nearest the cream cheese, then fold the other half down and seal the edges, making a triangle shape. Seal the edges tightly, but try to leave small gaps at the corners so the triangles will not expand so much that they burst.
3. Drop several wontons into oil at a time. Turn over when the edges start to brown and cook for another minute or two. Set on paper towels to drain, then serve hot with sweet-and-sour sauce.

3. GUACAMOLE DIP

This alternative recipe is somewhat simpler, but gives an extremely tasty Guacamole which is great with tortilla chips or vegetables, or can be used in enchiladas, etc. It also avoids messing about with messy tomatoes, or coriander, which some people do not like the taste of. I have tried many guacamole recipes over the years, this is both the simplest and in my opinion, the tastiest I know.

Ingredients

- 3 whole avocados, ripe but not over-ripe
- 1 lime
- 3 cloves of garlic
- 2 or 3 whole red chili peppers
- Salt

Procedure

1. Prepare avocados by halving and removing the stone (the simplest way to do this is to hold the avocado in the palm of your hand and strike the stone squarely and firmly with a chef's knife - the knife will then pull the stone out easily. If it doesn't come out easily, the avocado isn't ripe enough).
2. Keep one-half avocado back, skin and blend the rest using a hand-held food processor, add the juice of the lime, finely chop chilies and garlic, add and blend a bit longer.
3. Add generous salt to taste.
4. Finally roughly chop avocado half kept back and add to paste to give chunky texture. Resulting dip will keep for several days in a fridge, shouldn't brown too much if covered (the lime juice will act as an antioxidant as well as giving a nice flavor), but in general will be found to disappear very rapidly by enthusiastic consumers!

4. QUESADILLAS

Ingredients

- 2 flour tortilla, 6" (15cm), corn tortillas can be used in a pinch at home, but may not hold together or work as well as flour.
- 1/3 cup meltable cheese
- 1/4 cup Filling (see below)
- Cooking Spray

Procedure

1. Warm both tortillas in the microwave to the point of flexibility, at least, keeping one warm.
2. Preheat a frying pan or griddle (medium-low heat), seasoned with oil or cooking spray. Drop in the first tortilla.
3. Drop on it shredded cheese (typically Monterey Jack cheese).

4. Quickly add, and spread out, almost to the edges, any combination of the fillings listed below (or whatever additional ingredients you would like), ideally warmed and very well drained.
5. Allow the cheese to melt. The tortilla may brown in spots but it should not be cooked to the point of changing color substantially.
6. Press the other tortilla over the top of the tortilla in the pan, making sure it sticks a bit.
7. Flip the quesadilla and allow to warm until it joins as a unit.
8. Remove from pan, cut in 1/8ths.
9. Eat immediately, or, if you need to serve a bigger group, remove to a fairly low temperature 'keep warm' area, below the melting temperature of the cheese.

Quesadillas are usually not very good reheated.

Filings

- salsa
- sarza criolla
- chili peppers
- Chopped tomatoes and cilantro
- Cooked meat or seafood
- Fresh spinach--washed and torn into small pieces
- Black beans--canned, rinsed and well drained
- A fairly traditional filling would be grilled chicken, beef or pork, finely minced, sprinkled with a teaspoon of finely minced onion and half of teaspoon of cilantro, with a small amount of some lime squeezed on top.

5. EASY NACHOS

Ingredients

- 12 oz (360 g) bag tortilla chips
- 1 lb (450 g) Cheddar cheese, grated
- 1/3 cup (80 ml) chopped canned peeled green chilies (optional)
- 1/2 cup (about 120 ml) chopped onion (optional)

Procedure

1. Preheat the oven to 400°F (200°C). Lay the tortilla chips on a Cookie Sheet.
2. Toss together the cheese, chilies, and onion; sprinkle over the tortilla chips.
3. Bake for about 2 minutes, or until the cheese has melted.
4. Serve hot.

6. SCALLOP CEVICHE

Ingredients

- 1 pound (450 g) bay scallops
- 1/2 cup (125 mL) lemon juice (about 3-4 lemons)
- 4 red bell peppers, roasted, peeled and seeded
- 2 tablespoons (30 mL) balsamic vinegar
- 2 tablespoons (30 mL) extra-virgin olive oil
- 1/2 teaspoon (2.5 mL) cayenne pepper, ground
- Salt, to taste
- 1 avocado, peeled and sliced

Procedure

1. In a non-reactive bowl, combine the scallops and lemon juice, add more juice as needed to cover the scallops. Refrigerate, covered, and stir often for 2 hours, until the scallops become opaque.

2. For the sauce, add the bell peppers, vinegar, oil, cayenne, and salt into a food processor or blender, and purée.

3. To serve, spoon the sauce onto individual plates, drain the scallops and place on the sauce. Garnish with slices of avocado.

Serves 4 as a main dish, or as an appetizer.

7. SPINACH ARTICHOKE DIP

Formal or informal, Spinach Artichoke Dip is a great appetizer for any party. It is quick and easy taking very little time to prepare. The dip may be served with a variety of crackers, bread, or chips.

Ingredients

- 16 ounces (450g) cream cheese
- 3/4 cup (180ml) heavy cream (use half milk, if desired)
- 1/3 cup (80ml) grated Parmesan cheese
- 1/4 teaspoon (60ml) garlic powder
- 16 ounces (450g) frozen cut leaf spinach, thawed and well drained
- 1 can quarter artichoke hearts, rinsed and well drained
- 2/3 cup (160ml) shredded Monterey Jack cheese
- 1 cup prepared (240ml) salsa
- Crackers or tortilla chips, for serving

Procedure

1.   In a food processor fitted with a metal blade, process the cream cheese, cream, Parmesan cheese, and garlic powder until smooth and creamy. Add the spinach and process until thoroughly mixed. Add the artichokes and process just until coarsely chopped.

2.   Turn the mixture into a 3 1/2-quart electric slow cooker; smooth the top.

3.   Cover and cook on the high heat setting 1-1/4 to 1-1/2 hours, until hot in the center. Sprinkle the top evenly with the Jack cheese and spoon the salsa in a ring around the inside edges of the slow cooker. Cover and continue heating on high 15 minutes longer, or until the cheese is melted. Reduce the heat to the low setting and serve warm with crackers or tortilla chips for dipping. Refrigerate any leftovers.

8. WING THING

Ingredients

- 5 lb. chicken wings (tips removed)
- 1 c. onions, chopped
- 2 garlic cloves
- 3 Tbsp. olive oil
- 2 Tbsp. honey
- 1/3 c. olive oil
- 1 Tbsp. curry powder
- 1 Tbsp. chili powder
- 1 tsp. pepper
- 2/3 c. soy sauce
- 1/3 c. lime juice

Preparation

1. Saute onion and garlic in 3 tablespoons olive oil, then add remaining ingredients.
2. Heat together until warm.
3. Layer chicken wings in one layer in large flat baking dish/pan.
4. Pour sauce over wings and bake 1 hour at 375°.
5. Turn wings over at 30 minutes. Enjoy.
6. The sauce can also be used for a whole chicken or to marinate breasts too!

9. SWEET AND SOUR WINGS

Ingredients

- 3 lb. chicken wings
- 1 tsp. salt
- 1 c. cornstarch

- 3 eggs, beaten
- 1/4 c. soy sauce
- 1/2 c. vinegar
- 1/2 c. sugar
- 3 Tbsp. catsup
- 1/2 tsp. salt
- 1/2 c. red currant jelly
- 2 Tbsp. lemon juice

Preparation

1. Fry wings in deep fat, after dipping in cornstarch and egg, about 5 minutes.
2. Combine rest of ingredients and heat to boiling, stirring constantly.
3. Lower heat and simmer 10 minutes.
4. Pour over chicken. Bake at 350° for about 45 minutes. (Wing tips may be removed before cooking.)

10. BUFFALO WINGS

Ingredients

- 24 chicken wings (about 4 lb.)
- salt and pepper
- 4 c. safflower oil
- 1 stick corn oil margarine
- 4 Tbsp. (1/4 c.) Frank's Louisiana hot sauce (try Ferrante's, Durkee's or Nance's if you can't find Frank's)
- 2 tsp. white vinegar

Preparation

1. Sprinkle wings with salt and pepper.
2. Heat oil in deep fryer or heavy pot.
3. When hot, add half of the wings and cook 8 to 10 minutes.
4. When wings are golden, remove to warm paper towel-lined platter. Cook remaining wings.
5. Meanwhile, melt margarine in deep saucepan. Add Nance's sauce (or Frank's or whoever) and vinegar. Heat and stir one minute longer. Put some wings in a saucepan. Cover and shake until they are evenly coated. Repeat with the remainder. Serve with chilled celery sticks and Blue cheese dressing.

11. CHICKPEA DIP

Ingredients

- 1 (20 oz.) can chickpeas

- 1/2 tsp. salt
- ground black pepper
- 1 Tbsp. safflower oil
- 1 large clove garlic, minced
- 1/2 tsp. sesame seed
- 2 Tbsp. lemon juice

Preparation

1. Drain the chickpeas thoroughly, reserving the liquid.
2. Combine the chickpeas with the other ingredients in a blender jar.
3. Blend until creamy. If necessary, add some of the liquid from the chickpeas to reach the desired consistency.
4. Serve chilled and sprinkle with chopped parsley as a dip for raw vegetables, or as a spread.

12. 8 LAYER MEXICAN DIP

Ingredients

- 1 can refried beans (Old El Paso with green chilies, standard sized can)
- 8 oz. avocado dip (use a brand that is already prepared)
- 8 oz. sour cream
- 1 medium size tomato, chopped (let the juice drain off the tomato after it is chopped, otherwise it might thin the dip too much)
- 8 oz. jar Picante sauce
- sliced jalapeno peppers, as many, as desired
- 3 oz. chopped olives
- 8 oz. grated Cheddar cheese

Preparation

1. Chop your tomato first, so it can be draining while you are fixing the first three layers.
2. Layer the ingredients on a large platter in the order listed. You might want to make this dip in a round dish, about the size of a pizza pan. It will end up looking kind of like a pizza.

13. FRENCH ONION DIP

Ingredients

- 1 pkg. Lipton onion soup mix
- 1 (16 oz.) sour cream
- 1 pkg. Ranch dressing mix
- 1 (16 oz.) sour cream

Preparation

1. Mix the Lipton onion soup mix to the sour cream. Chill for 2 to 3 hours. Serve with chips.
2. Mix Ranch dressing mix with sour cream. Chill for 2 to 3 hours. Serve with vegetables.

14. BEST SPINACH DIP

Ingredients

- 1 (10 oz.) pkg. frozen spinach, thawed and drained
- 3 green onions
- 1 (8 oz.) can sliced water chestnuts
- 1 c. Dukes mayonnaise
- 1 1/2 c. sour cream
- 1 pkg. Knorr vegetable soup mix

Preparation

1. Thaw frozen chopped spinach and squeeze dry.
2. Stir soup mix, sour cream, and mayonnaise until blended.
3. Stir in spinach, water chestnuts (chopped) and chopped green onions.
4. Cover and chill 2 hours.
5. Stir before serving. Makes 4 cups.

15. 4TH OF JULY DIP

Ingredients

- 8 oz. pkg. cream cheese
- 1/3 c. French dressing
- 3 Tbsp. ketchup
- 1 1/2 Tbsp. grated onion

Preparation

1. Soften cream cheese and add rest of ingredients.
2. Mix well. Chill to blend flavors. Serve with veggies.

16. 7-UP CINNAMON AND SOUR CREAM FRUIT DIP

Ingredients

- 1 (8 oz.) pkg. sour cream
- 2 Tbsp. 7-Up

- 2 Tbsp. brown sugar
- 1 tsp. cinnamon

Preparation

1. In a small bowl, combine all ingredients and mix well.
2. Cover; refrigerate 1 to 2 hours before serving to blend flavors.
3. Serve with fresh fruits.

17. SEAFOOD CHEESE BALLS

Ingredients

- 1/2 Cup of Bottled Chili Sauce
- 1 tsp. of Horseradish
- 1 tsp. Worcestershire Sauce
- 1/4 tsp. of Tabasco Sauce
- 2 Tbsp. of Lemon Juice
- 1 tsp. of Chopped Chives
- 1/4 tsp. of Parsley
- 1 tsp. of Salt
- 1 - 8 oz. pkg. of Cream Cheese (Softened)
- 1 Sm Can of Small Shrimp
- 1 or 2 Tbsp. of Lemon Juice

Preparation

1. Mix first 8 ingredients together and refrigerate to chill.
2. Mix next 3 ingredients together and form into a ball.
3. Chill the cheese ball for 3 hours.
4. When ready to serve, pour the sauce over the cheese ball and serve with your favorite crackers.

18. CREAMY SEAFOOD DIP

Ingredients

- 1 (8 oz.) pkg. Delicaseas Sea Stix salad style crab meat
- 1 (8 oz.) pkg. cream cheese
- 1/2 c. salad dressing
- 1/4 c. chopped celery
- 1/4 c. chopped onion
- 2 Tbsp. lemon juice

Preparation

1. Blend together cream cheese, salad dressing, and lemon juice.
2. Add salad mix, onion, and celery.
3. Mix well. Serve with crackers. Makes 2 1/2 cups.

19. PARTY SEAFOOD DIP

Ingredients

- 1 (8 oz.) pkg. cream cheese, soft
- 1 jar Nalley seafood sauce
- 1 can shrimp or crab crackers

Preparation

1. Put cream cheese on a serving dish.
2. Pile shrimp or crab on top. Pour on seafood sauce.
3. Serve with a variety of crackers.

20. SWEET AND SOUR MEATBALLS OR WAIKIKI MEATBALLS

Ingredients

- 1 1/2 lb. ground beef
- 2/3 c. cracker crumbs
- 1/3 c. minced onion
- 1 egg
- 1 1/2 tsp. salt
- 1/4 tsp. ginger
- 1/4 c. milk
- 1 Tbsp. shortening
- 2 Tbsp. cornstarch
- 1/2 c. brown sugar, packed
- 1 (13 1/2 oz.) can pineapple tidbits, drained (reserve syrup)*
- 1/3 c. vinegar
- 1 Tbsp. soy sauce
- 1/3 c. chopped green pepper

Preparation

*I usually double this recipe so there is enough gravy.

1. Mix meat, crumbs, onion, egg, salt, ginger and milk.
2. Shape mixture by rounded tablespoons into balls.
3. Melt shortening in large skillet. Brown and cook meatballs.

4. Remove meatballs; keep warm. Pour fat from skillet. Mix cornstarch and sugar.
5. Stir in reserved pineapple syrup, vinegar, and soy sauce until smooth.
6. Pour into skillet; cook over medium heat, stirring constantly, until mixture thickens and boils.
7. Boil and stir 1 minute.
8. Add meatballs, pineapple tidbits, and green pepper; heat through.

21. "COCKTAIL MEATBALLS"

Ingredients

- 1 1/2 lb. ground beef
- 1/4 c. milk
- 1 egg
- 1 tsp. salt
- 1/4 tsp. thyme
- 1 c. bread crumbs (Italian flavor)
- 1/2 c. chopped onion
- 1/4 tsp. nutmeg

Preparation

1. Combine all ingredients and form into meatballs.
2. Bake 25 to 30 minutes at 350°.

22. SAUCE

Ingredients

- 1/2 c. diced onion
- 1 c. tomato soup (canned)
- 2 Tbsp. brown sugar
- 1 Tbsp. Worcestershire sauce
- 2 Tbsp. butter
- 2 c. barbecue sauce
- 1 Tbsp. vinegar
- 1 Tbsp. dry mustard

Preparation

Combine all and heat to bubble. Add meatballs. Easy, easy, easy!

23. "SWEETISH" MEATBALLS AND SAUCE

Ingredients

- 1 1/2 lb. ground beef
- 1 slice bread
- 2 eggs
- 1/4 c. finely chopped onion
- 1/2 chopped clove garlic
- 3 Tbsp. Parmesan cheese
- 1/4 tsp. oregano
- 3 c. brown sugar
- 1 1/2 c. ketchup

Preparation

Meatballs:

1. Soak bread in water or milk to cover.
2. When completely soaked, wring liquid from bread.
3. Add to meat and other ingredients, except brown sugar and ketchup.
4. Mix well. Shape into meatballs.
5. Bake, covered, for 30 minutes at 350°.

Sauce:

1. Combine brown sugar and ketchup in a saucepan.
2. Mix well. Bring to a boil over high heat.
3. Reduce heat and simmer, with meatballs, added, for 20 minutes.

24. BACON STIX

Ingredients

- 6 slices bacon
- 6 thin breadsticks (any flavor)
- 1/4 c. grated Parmesan cheese

Preparation

1. Dredge one side of each bacon strip in cheese.
2. Roll the coated bacon diagonally around bread sticks, cheese side inward.
3. Place sticks on a paper towel-lined platter.
4. Microwave at High for 4 to 6 minutes until bacon begins to brown.
5. Rotate plate once. Roll each stick in cheese again.
6. You might want to cut the bacon in half and wrap around stick pretzels. These make great appetizers.

25. PRALINE STIX

Ingredients

- 3/4 c. sugar
- 2 sticks oleo
- 1 pkg. graham crackers
- 1 c. chopped nuts

Preparation

1. Line a cookie sheet with foil (use a cookie sheet with sides).
2. Boil sugar and oleo for 2 minutes.
3. Separate crackers, place in rows on foil.
4. Pour sauce over crackers and sprinkle with nuts.
5. Bake 8 to 10 minutes at 325°. Peel crackers off foil.

26. SWEET PICKLE STIX

Ingredients

- Cucumbers
- 3 3/4 c. Vinegar
- 3 c. Sugar
- 3 tbsp. Canning salt
- 4 1/2 tsp. Celery seed
- 4 1/2 tsp. Turmeric
- 3/4 tsp. Mustard seed

Preparation

Wash cucumbers and cut into spears. Pour boiling water over cucumbers and let stand for 3 to 5 hours. Drain. Pack into sterilized jars. Mix all ingredients to make a solution (except cucumbers). Boil solution 5 minutes. Pour over cucumber sticks. Put in boiling water bath for 5 minutes. Makes approximately 5 to 7 quarts.

SALAD RECIPES

27. TOSSED ITALIAN SALAD

Ingredients

- 4 c. Fresh spinach, torn
- 2 c. Red leaf lettuce, torn
- 1 medium green or sweet yellow pepper, cut into strips (1 c.)
- 2/3 c. Thinly sliced radishes
- 1 small red onion, sliced and separated into rings
- 2 tbsp. Red wine vinegar
- 4 tsp. Olive oil or salad oil
- 1/2 tsp. Garlic salt
- 1/2 tsp. Dried oregano, crushed
- 2 tbsp. Grated parmesan cheese
- Ground pepper (if desired)

Preparation

Salad: Place spinach, lettuce, pepper strips, radish slices and onion rings in a large salad bowl and toss lightly.

Dressing: In a screw-top jar combine vinegar, olive oil, garlic salt, oregano and 1 tablespoon water. Cover and shake well to mix.

Pour dressing over salad. Toss lightly to coat. Sprinkle Parmesan cheese over salad and toss lightly. Sprinkle with ground pepper (if desired). Serve immediately. Makes 4 servings.

Per Serving: 83 Calories, 6 g. Fat, 2 mg. Cholesterol and 364 mg. Sodium.

28. CARROT SALAD

Ingredients

- 1 (8 oz.) Can crushed pineapple (juice packed), drained (reserve 2 tbsp. Juice)
- 2 c. Shredded carrot
- 1/2 c. Sliced celery or chopped green pepper
- 1/2 tsp. Finely shredded lemon peel
- 1 tbsp. Lemon juice
- 1 tsp. Sugar or brown sugar
- 1/4 tsp. Salt
- Dash of ground ginger
- 4 lettuce leaves (optional)

Preparation

1. In a medium mixing bowl, combine drained pineapple, reserved pineapple juice, carrot, celery or green pepper, lemon peel, lemon juice, sugar, salt, and ginger.
2. Toss to coat well. Cover and chill for 2 to 24 hours, stirring occasionally.
3. Serve on lettuce-lined plates, if desired. Makes 4 servings.

29. POPPY-SEED FRUIT SALAD

Ingredients

- 1 (10 1/2 oz.) Can mandarin orange sections (water packed), drained
- 1 (8 oz.) Can pineapple tidbits (juice packed), drained (reserve 1 tbsp. Juice)
- 1 1/2 c. Small strawberries, cut in half, or seedless red grapes
- 1 medium apple, cored and cut into bite-size pieces
- 1/2 c. Pineapple low-fat yogurt
- 1/2 tsp. Poppy seed
- Lettuce leaves

Preparation

1. In a medium mixing bowl combine orange sections, pineapple, strawberries or grapes and apple. Toss lightly to mix.
2. In a small bowl stir together yogurt, poppy seed, and reserved pineapple juice.
3. To Serve Line salad plates with the lettuce leaves. Arrange fruit mixture on lettuce and drizzle dressing over fruit. Makes 5 or 6 servings.

30. GRANNY'S POTATO SALAD

Ingredients

- 3 pounds California long white potatoes
- 3 hard-boiled eggs, chopped
- 1 medium onion, minced
- 3/4 cup mayonnaise
- 1/4 cup sweet pickle juice (from a jar of pickles)
- 1 tablespoon dried parsley
- 1/2 teaspoon celery seed
- 3/4 tablespoon sugar
- salt
- pepper
- paprika

Procedure

1. Cut unpeeled potatoes in half and cook until they are tender when tested with a knife. Do not overcook.
2. Peel the potatoes by scraping them lightly with a knife and cut them into 1/2 inch (1.25 cm) cubes.
3. Place potatoes in a large bowl and let them come to room temperature.
4. In a small bowl, combine the mayonnaise, pickle juice, and sugar and stir until smooth.
5. Add the mayonnaise mixture, minced onion, parsley, celery seed and chopped eggs to the potatoes.
6. Add salt and pepper to taste. Stir lightly to combine.
7. Place in a large serving bowl and sprinkle with paprika.
8. Cover and refrigerate until ready to serve.

31. "MEN LIKE IT" SALAD

- **Ingredients**
- 1 small box lime jello
- 1 small pkg. Cream cheese (3 oz.)
- 1 small can crush pineapple with liquid

- 1 c. Diced celery
- 1/2 c. Chopped nuts
- 1 3/4 c. Hot water

Preparation

1. Mix jello and water.
2. Soften cream cheese and blend into pineapple.
3. Add celery and nuts.
4. When jello slightly congeals, add other ingredients and refrigerate until firm.

32. CRAB AND CORN SALAD

Ingredients

- 8 oz imitation crab meat
- 16 oz canned whole kernel sweet corn
- 1/2 cup mayonnaise
- 1-2 green onions
- (optional) shredded cheese (to taste)

Procedure

1. Chop imitation crab meat and green onions.
2. Combine the above, corn and mayonnaise in an appropriately sized bowl.
3. Mix well
4. (Optional) Add shredded cheese to taste and mix again

33. SPICY BLACK BEAN SALAD

Ingredients

- 2 cups canned black beans, rinsed and drained
- 1 tbs salt
- 1 tbs freshly ground black pepper
- 1 1/2 tbs chili oil
- 1/2 tbs vegetable oil
- 2 tsp rice vinegar
- 1 1/2 tsp soy sauce
- 1 Thai bird chile, minced

Procedure

1. Heat oils in a large skillet over medium-high heat. Add all ingredients and toss; cook just until heated through.
2. Serve immediately as a side dish or cool slightly and serve as a salad.

34. STEAK ARUGULA

Ingredients

- 2 cups arugula (rocket)
- 2 (6-8 ounce) beef ribeye steaks
- Salt and freshly ground black pepper
- 3/4 cup minus 1 Tbs extra-virgin olive oil, divided
- 1/4 cup red wine vinegar
- 1 1/4 tsp Dijon mustard
- 5 rashers bacon, cut into 1 1/2 inch pieces and crisp-cooked
- 2 tbs rendered bacon fat

Procedure

1. Brush steaks with 1 tbs olive oil. Sprinkle liberally with salt and freshly ground black pepper.
2. Grill over very high heat 1 minute. Twist 90 degrees, cook for another 1 minute, then flip and repeat 1 more time.
3. Move to medium heat and cook, turning often, until desired "doneness" is achieved. (145°F for medium-rare, 160°F for medium, and 170°F for toast)
4. Refrigerate steaks until chilled.
5. Combine remaining oil and bacon fat. In another bowl, combine mustard and vinegar. Slowly stream in olive oil while whisking continuously.
6. Slice steaks thinly across the grain at a 45-degree angle. Toss together remaining ingredients and dressing in your serving bowl and refrigerate until chilled. Serve cold.

35. TURKEY BACON SALAD

Ingredients

- 1 head of lettuce
- 2 cups of carrots, shredded
- 1 cup of sliced olives
- 4 to 5 slices of deli turkey
- 4 to 5 slices of cooked bacon

Procedure

1. Cook bacon completely.
2. Remove excess grease by pressing cooked bacon on a disposable paper towel.
3. Chop bacon strips into small pieces.
4. Clean lettuce, carrots, and olives.
5. Shred lettuce either by hand or with a preparing knife.
6. Lay desired amount of lettuce in clean bowl, a minimum of 2 cups recommended.
7. Roll deli turkey to form a slender shape.
8. Slowly slice turkey into circular shapes.

9. Pile carrots, olive, bacon, and turkey on lettuce.
10. Top off with your favorite dressing.

36. PASTA-CRAB SALAD

Ingredients

- 2 oz. Vermicelli
- 1 (6 oz.) Pkg. Frozen crab meat
- 1/2 c. Thinly sliced celery
- 1/4 c. Low-calorie mayonnaise
- 1 tbsp. Sliced pimiento, drained
- 1 tbsp. Minced green onion
- 1/4 tsp. Salt
- 1/8 tsp. Pepper

Preparation

1. Break vermicelli into 2-inch lengths.
2. Cook according to directions.
3. Rinse with cold running water and drain well.
4. In a medium bowl, toss vermicelli with remaining ingredients.
5. Cover and chill 20 minutes. Makes 2 servings.

37. CALIFORNIA CHICKEN SALAD

Ingredients

- 3 Tbsp. Lemon juice
- 1 c. Diced, cooked chicken
- 1/2 c. Finely diced apples
- 1/2 c. Chopped ripe olives
- 1/2 c. Diced celery
- 2 tsp. Mayonnaise thinned with 2 Tbsp. Cream (sweet or sour)

Preparation

1. Sprinkle lemon juice over chicken and apples, mixing lightly.
2. Combine remaining ingredients, using only enough mayonnaise to moisten.
3. Add chicken and apples and toss together lightly. Serve cold.

38. PEACH WEDDING RING SALAD

Ingredients

- 1 (No. 2 1/2) can cling peaches
- 2 pkg. Lemon gelatin
- 1 1/2 c. Hot water
- 1/4 c. Chopped walnuts
- 8 to 10 maraschino cherries
- 1 (12 oz.) Ginger ale (1 1/2 c.)
- Mayo (optional)
- Salad greens (optional)

Preparation

1. Drain peaches well. Overlap slices in 1 1/2-quart ring mold.
2. Outline ring with quartered cherries.
3. Dissolve gelatin in hot water. Add ginger ale.
4. Spoon a little gelatin into the mold around the fruit.
5. Chill remaining gelatin until thickened.
6. Beat until fluffy with rotary beater.
7. Chop remaining peaches; fold into gelatin with nuts.
8. Turn into the mold over clear layer. Chill until firm. Unmold on salad greens.
9. Serve with mayo (optional). Can also be molded in an oblong Pyrex dish.
10. Cut into squares and use a spatula to remove and turn over to see peaches and cherries.

39. SALAD FOR LOVERS

Ingredients

- 1 lb. Can baked beans, drained (remove pork)
- 6 hard-boiled eggs, chopped coarsely
- 3 to 4 slices cooked bacon, crumbled
- 1/4 c. Caesar salad dressing

Preparation

1. Drain beans and remove pork.
2. Add chopped eggs, crumbled bacon and dressing.
3. Best if made the night before or a few hours before serving.

MEAT RECIPE

40. BARBECUE LOVER'S CHICKEN

Ingredients

- 1 can onion soup
- 1 can tomato soup
- 2 tbsp. Cornstarch
- 1/4 tsp. Garlic juice
- 1/4 cup vinegar
- 5 tbsp. Brown sugar
- 1 tbsp. Worcestershire sauce
- 1/8 tsp. Hot pepper sauce

Preparation

1. In a bowl combine all ingredients.
2. In a skillet, slowly brown chicken in butter (about 25 minutes).
3. Add sauce mixture.
4. Cover and cook over low heat 20 minutes. Stir often. Serve with rice.

41. "ARNI PSITO" - LEG OF LAMB

Ingredients

- 1 leg of lamb
- 4 to 5 cloves garlic, halved or quartered (optional)
- 3/4 stick butter
- 1/4 to 1/2 c. lemon juice (use more or less according to personal preference)
- 1 tsp. oregano

Preparation

1. Make holes in meat with a sharp knife and insert cloves of garlic throughout the lamb.
2. Place in roasting pan with just enough water to barely cover the bottom of the pan.
3. Bake at 350° to 375° oven for about 30 to 45 minutes.
4. Remove from oven. Melt butter; add lemon juice and oregano.
5. Pour lemon mixture over lamb and bake for about 1 1/2 hours, basting every few minutes with sauce.
6. Remove from oven and let set a few minutes.
7. Cut meat from bone and place meat in juice.
8. Continue baking in oven until fork-tender.

42. CALIFORNIA GRILLED CHICKEN

Ingredients

- 3/4 c. balsamic vinegar
- 1 tsp. garlic powder
- 2 tbsp. honey
- 2 tbsp. extra-virgin olive oil
- 2 tsp. Italian seasoning
- kosher salt
- Freshly ground black pepper
- 4 boneless skinless chicken breasts
- 4 slices mozzarella
- 4 slices avocado
- 4 slices tomato
- 2 tbsp. sliced basil

- Balsamic glaze, for drizzling

Preparation

1. In a small bowl, whisk together balsamic vinegar, garlic powder, honey, oil, and Italian seasoning and season with salt and pepper. Pour over chicken breasts and marinate 20 minutes.
2. Heat grill to medium high. Grill chicken until internal temperature reaches 170°F on an instant-read thermometer.
3. Top chicken with mozzarella, avocado, and tomato and cover grill to melt, 2 minutes.
4. Garnish with basil and drizzle with balsamic glaze.

43. CROCK-POT BARBECUE TURKEY LEGS

Ingredients

- 4 uncooked turkey drumsticks or thighs
- salt and pepper
- 1/4 c. molasses
- 1/4 c. vinegar
- 1/4 c. catsup
- 2 Tbsp. Worcestershire sauce
- 1/2 tsp. hickory smoke salt
- 1 Tbsp. instant minced onion

Preparation

1. Sprinkle turkey with salt and pepper.
2. Place in the slow cooking pot
3. Combine remaining ingredients; pour over turkey.
4. Cover and cook on low for 5 to 7 minutes.
5. If turkey legs are small, serve 1 thigh or drumstick per person.
6. If large, slice off cooked meat and serve with sauce. Serves 4 to 6.

44. DEEP FAT-FRIED FROG LEGS

Ingredients

- 2 eggs
- 1 c. milk
- 1/2 tsp. cayenne
- 1 tsp. salt
- 1/2 tsp. garlic powder
- 1 c. flour
- 8 pairs frog legs

- 1 qt. cooking oil
- 1/2 c. flour
- 1/2 c. cornmeal
- salt and pepper
- 1/4 tsp. garlic powder
- 1/2 tsp. onion powder
- 1/2 tsp. cayenne

Preparation

1. Beat together the eggs, milk, and seasonings.
2. Gradually stir in the flour. Set this aside and prepare the dredge by mixing together the flour, cornmeal, salt, pepper, garlic powder, onion powder, and cayenne.
3. Add the oil to a deep fat fryer and heat.
4. Prepare the frog legs by dipping them in the egg-milk preparation and then coating them with the dry ingredients.
5. Fry the legs, one pair at a time, until golden brown.
6. Remove and drain on paper towels.

45. PILAF STUFFED CHICKEN LEGS

Ingredients

- 1 medium onion, chopped
- 1 c. uncooked rice
- 2 Tbsp. margarine
- 1 tsp. curry powder
- 1/4 c. currants
- 2 1/2 c. chicken broth
- 8 whole chicken legs (thighs attached)

Preparation

1. Saute onion and uncooked rice in mayonnaise until onion is tender.
2. Blend in the curry powder and currants.
3. Stir in broth. Cover and cook about 20 minutes or until rice is tender. Let cool.
4. To stuff, carefully lift up the skin of thigh.
5. Spoon about 2/3 cup of rice mixture under skin of each leg, keeping skin and membrane intact as much as possible.
6. Use fingers to push rice down leg.
7. Wipe away excess rice and pull the skin over the opening.
8. Arrange in greased pan.
9. Cover and refrigerate until baking.
10. Brush with oil. Bake uncovered 50 minutes or until tender in 325° oven.

46. TANGY CHICKEN LEGS

Ingredients

- 1 c. brewed coffee
- 1 c. ketchup
- 1/2 c. sugar
- 1/2 c. Worcestershire sauce
- 1/4 c. vinegar
- 1/8 tsp. pepper
- 8 grilled or broiled chicken leg quarters

Preparation

1. In a saucepan, combine the first six ingredients.
2. Bring to a boil. Reduce heat.
3. Simmer, uncovered, for 30 to 35 minutes or until thickened, stirring occasionally.
4. Brush over cooked chicken. Yield: 8 servings (1 1/2 cups barbecue sauce).

47. "MOUTHWATERING" BAKED CHICKEN BREASTS

Ingredients

- 2 double chicken breasts, deboned and split
- 1 c. sour cream
- 2 Tbsp. lemon juice
- 1 tsp. celery salt
- 2 Tbsp. Worcestershire sauce
- 3/4 tsp. paprika
- 1 tsp. garlic salt
- 1/2 tsp. salt
- 1/8 tsp. pepper
- 1 c. dry bread crumbs
- 1/4 c. margarine

Preparation

1. Combine sour cream with spices, juice and Worcestershire sauce.
2. Coat each piece of chicken in mixture and let stand, covered, in the refrigerator overnight or all day.
3. Roll chicken pieces in bread crumbs, coating well.
4. Arrange in single layer in baking pan.
5. Melt margarine and spoon over a cool piece of chicken.
6. Bake in 350° oven, uncovered, 1 hour or until golden (if baked in Pyrex dish, reduce heat slightly).

48. Philly Cheese steak Foil Packs

Ingredients

- 1 lb. flank steak, thinly sliced
- 2 bell peppers, thinly sliced
- 1/2 onion, thinly sliced
- 2 cloves garlic, minced
- 2 tbsp. Italian seasoning
- 2 tbsp. extra-virgin olive oil
- kosher salt
- Freshly ground black pepper
- 4 slices provolone
- Chopped fresh parsley, for garnish

Preparation

1. Heat grill to medium-high. In a large bowl, toss together steak, peppers, onion, garlic, Italian seasoning, and olive oil and season with salt and pepper.
2. Place steak mixture in foil packs. Fold up packs and grill, 10 minutes.
3. Open packs, top with provolone, and cover grill to melt, 2 minutes.
4. Garnish with parsley and serve

49. ALMOND CHICKEN BREAST

Ingredients

- 2 eggs, lightly beaten
- 1/2 c. half and half
- 1/2 c. milk
- 1 tsp. salt
- 1 tsp. Hungarian paprika
- 3/4 c. all-purpose flour
- 3 whole chicken breasts, skinned, boned and flattened
- all-purpose flour for dredging
- 1 c. ground blanched almonds
- 1/2 c. dried bread crumbs
- 8 Tbsp. butter
- 1/4 c. sliced almonds
- 2 Tbsp. melted butter

Preparation

1. Fifteen to 30 minutes before you're ready to bake, preheat oven to 350°.
2. Lightly butter bottom of the ovenproof baking dish.

3. In a bowl, combine eggs, half and half, milk, salt, paprika, and flour; beat to form a pasty batter. Marinate chicken breast in the batter for at least 1 hour in the refrigerator.
4. Combine ground almonds and breadcrumbs. Spread evenly over a sheet of waxed paper. Remove chicken breast from marinade; drain.
5. Dredge in flour, then coat with breadcrumb mixture. Allow setting 15 minutes.
6. In a heavy skillet or saute pan over medium heat, melt butter.
7. Add chicken breast and cook for about 2 to 3 minutes on each side, until lightly browned.
8. Place in prepared baking dish, sprinkle with sliced almonds and drizzle with melted butter. Bake 15 minutes or until crisp and golden brown.

50. GRILLED HONEY-LIME CHICKEN WITH PINEAPPLE SALSA

Ingredients

- Juice of 4 limes, divided
- 1/4 c. extra-virgin olive oil
- 1/4 c. plus 1 tbsp. chopped fresh cilantro
- 2 tsp. honey
- kosher salt
- 1 lb. boneless skinless chicken breasts
- 2 c. chopped pineapple
- 1 avocado, diced
- 1/4 red onion, diced
- Freshly ground black pepper

Preparation

1. Make Marinade: In a large bowl, whisk together juice of 3 limes, olive oil, 1/4 cup cilantro and honey and season with salt.
2. Add chicken to a large Ziploc bag or baking dish and pour over marinade. Let marinate in the refrigerator at least 3 hours, or up to overnight.
3. When ready to grill, heat grill to high. Oil grates and add chicken, then grill until charred, 8 minutes per side.
4. Meanwhile, in a medium bowl, stir together pineapple, avocado, red onion, remaining lime juice, and remaining tablespoon cilantro. Season with salt and pepper.
5. Spoon salsa over chicken and serve.

51. QUEEN (GROUND BEEF) OR BEEF

Ingredients

- 1 lb. stew meat
- 1 big onion
- 4 cardamom
- 1/2 tsp. salt
- 1 Tbsp. fresh chopped ginger
- 1 Tbsp. garlic powder

- 1/2 tsp. chili powder
- 1 Tbsp. coriander powder
- 1/2 c. plain yogurt
- 1/4 c. vegetable oil

Preparation

1. Cut and fry the onion in vegetable oil until red. Add meat and other ingredients.
2. Let it cook on high heat for about 5 minutes, then turn the heat down.
3. Let it cook until the meat is tender.

52. "A-1" BEEF TENDERLOINS

Ingredients

- 1 pkg. lean beef cubes
- 1 Tbsp. butter or margarine
- 1/3 c. A.1. steak sauce
- 2 to 3 Tbsp. teriyaki sauce
- 1/2 green pepper
- 1/2 pkg. mushrooms
- 1 small onion, diced

Preparation

1. Cut beef cubes into bite-size pieces (partially freeze beef cubes for easier cutting).
2. Saute cubes in a frypan with butter or margarine, until tender.
3. Add steak sauce and teriyaki sauce to beef. Simmer 2 to 3 minutes.
4. Add pepper, mushrooms (cut into thin strips) and onion to beef.
5. Simmer an additional 5 minutes, or until vegetables are tender-crisp.
6. Serve over rice or noodles, or serve plain as a main dish.

53. "BEEF STROGANOFF"

Ingredients

- 3 lb. beef, sirloin, top round or tenderloin tips
- 1/4 c. flour
- 1 tsp. garlic powder
- 1/2 tsp. black pepper
- 6 Tbsp. oleo
- 1 1/4 c. chopped or minced onions
- 1/2 c. water
- 1 1/2 cans chicken soup (cream style)
- 1 1/2 lb. fresh mushrooms or 1 (1 lb.) can mushrooms

- 2 c. sour cream
- 1/2 tsp. nutmeg
- 1/2 c. dry sherry

Preparation

1. Cut meat 1 inch long by 1/4 inch thick.
2. Coat with flour, garlic, and pepper. Brown in a large skillet. Remove meat.
3. Brown onions in the same pan. Slowly stir in water, soup, and mushrooms.
4. Cook until hot. Add meat and simmer 20 to 30 minutes or until meat is tender.
5. Mix nutmeg, dry sherry, and sour cream together.
6. Add to mixture and serve. (If not thick enough, thicken with cornstarch and water mixture.)

54. AFRICAN BEEF STEW

Ingredients

- 2 tsp. vegetable oil
- 1 1/2 c. chopped onions
- 1 lb. lean ground beef
- 1 1/2 c. chicken broth
- 1/2 c. chunky or smooth peanut butter
- 1/4 c. tomato paste
- 1/2 tsp. salt
- 1/4 tsp. ground red pepper (cayenne) or to taste
- 2 1/2 c. frozen chunks butternut squash from 20 oz. bag

Preparation

1. Heat oil in a large, preferably nonstick skillet.
2. Stir in onions and cook over medium-high heat 4 to 5 minutes until translucent.
3. Add beef and cook 5 minutes, stirring with a fork to break up chunks, or until browned.
4. Drain off fat. Stir in broth, peanut butter, tomato paste, salt and red pepper until well blended (mixture will thicken).
5. Stir in squash, reduce heat, cover and simmer 5 to 7 minutes until squash is hot.
6. Uncover and simmer 5 minutes longer for flavors to blend.
7. Try this stew over rice with a side dish of steamed kale or collard greens.

55. SKINNY ORANGE CHICKEN

Ingredients

- 2 c. all-purpose flour
- 2 large Eggs, beaten
- 2 c. panko bread crumbs

- 1 lb. boneless skinless chicken breasts, cut into chunks
- kosher salt
- Freshly ground black pepper
- Juice and zest of 2 oranges
- 1/3 c. low-sodium soy sauce
- 1/4 c. honey
- 2 cloves garlic, minced
- 2 tsp. freshly grated ginger
- 2 tbsp. cornstarch
- 2 c. cooked jasmine rice
- Sesame seeds, for garnish
- Sliced green onions, for garnish

Preparation

1. Preheat oven to 400° and line a baking sheet with parchment.
2. Set up a dredging station with one bowl of flour, one of eggs, and one of panko. Dredge the chicken in flour, then coat in eggs and cover in panko. Season generously with salt and pepper.
3. Arrange chicken on parchment-lined baking sheet and bake until no longer pink, 18 to 20 minutes.
4. Meanwhile, make sauce: In a small saucepan over medium heat, combine orange juice, soy sauce, honey, garlic, ginger, and cornstarch. Whisk until combined and cook until thickened, about 5 minutes.
5. Transfer chicken to a large bowl and toss in orange sauce.
6. Serve over rice with orange zest, sesame seeds, and green onions.

56. ALL DAY BEEF STEW

Ingredients

- 2 lb. lean stew meat, cubed
- 1 lb. bag frozen mixed vegetables
- 4 carrots, sliced
- 2 onions, cut into chunks
- 2 stalks celery, sliced
- 1 (28 oz.) can whole tomatoes (undrained)
- 1/4 c. Minute tapioca
- 1 heaping tsp. instant coffee
- 1/4 tsp. thyme
- 1 tsp. oregano
- 1/2 tsp. salt
- dash of pepper
- 1 beef bouillon cube or 1 tsp. instant bouillon
- 1/2 c. water

Preparation

1. Put all ingredients into a large ovenproof pan. Mix and cover.
2. Cook in a preheated oven at 250° for 7 hours, at 300° for 5 hours or at 350° for 3 hours.
3. It makes its own gravy.

57. ALL BEEF BAKE SAUSAGE

Ingredients

- 3 lb. Lean ground beef
- 2 tbsp. Liquid smoke
- 1/4 tsp. Garlic salt
- 1 tsp. Mustard seed
- 3 tbsp. Meat curing salt
- 1 c. Water
- 1/4 tsp. Black pepper
- 1/2 tsp. Onion salt

Preparation

1. In a large bowl, mix all ingredients thoroughly.
2. Shape with hands into 3 rolls.
3. Place each roll on a sheet of heavy-duty aluminum foil, shiny side out. Refrigerate for 24 hours.
4. Place rolls, still wrapped, on a baking sheet and bake in 325° preheated oven for 1 hour and 15 minutes.
5. Cool and unwrap. Roll in fresh foil. Refrigerate or freeze until ready to use. Great for wild meat.

58. ALL MAN BEEF SANDWICH

Ingredients

- 2 all beef hot dogs
- 2 tbsp. Oleo

Preparation

1. Put oleo in a cast-iron skillet over medium heat.
2. Place 2 all beef hot dogs into oleo and heat to golden brown.
3. Put hot dogs into a warm bun with fresh onion and mustard.

59. A MAN'S DISH

Ingredients

- 1 can tuna
- 4 to 6 eggs, beaten
- Salt
- Pepper

Preparation

1. Open can of tuna and empty into the skillet (medium heat) or saucepan.
2. Heat tuna until hot and pour in beaten eggs.
3. Salt and pepper to taste. Cook until eggs are done.

60. A WORKING MAN'S CHOICE

Ingredients

- 2 lb. Hamburger
- 1 medium can green beans
- Salt and pepper
- 1 pkg. Taco seasoning mix
- Sliced swiss cheese
- 1 medium can corn
- Granulated garlic
- Seasoned salt
- 8 medium-sized potatoes, mashed
- 1 c. Stewed tomatoes

Preparation

1. Brown meat and seasoning to taste.
2. Add corn and green beans and mix well.
3. Pour into a 9 x 11-inch casserole dish with lid, then spread mashed potatoes over the top of meat evenly, then put sliced Swiss cheese over the top of everything.
4. Salt and pepper. Put the lid on and bake for 1 hour at 350° or until everything is hot throughout.
5. A change of pace: try Italian seasoning mix instead of taco.

61. EVERY MAN'S BEEF BURGUNDY

Ingredients

- 2 lbs. Chuck steak (1 inch thick)
- Instant unseasoned meat tenderizer
- 4 slices bacon
- Salt and pepper to taste
- 1 (10 1/2 oz.) Can beef broth
- 1 tbsp. Worcestershire sauce
- 1 c. Dry red wine
- 3/4 c. Water
- 2 cloves garlic, minced
- 1 bay leaf
- 1 large onion, quartered
- 4 medium carrots, cubed
- 1 (4 oz.) Can slice mushrooms, undrained

Preparation

1. Cut steak into 1-inch cubes; sprinkle with meat tenderizer, following label directions.
2. In a large skillet, cook bacon until crisp.
3. Remove bacon, crumble and set aside.
4. Quickly brown meat in bacon fat; drain off excess fat.
5. Season meat to taste with salt and pepper. Add broth, wine, water, garlic, bay leaf, and bacon.
6. Cover and simmer 50 minutes or until vegetables are tender.
7. Thicken liquid with thin flour and water paste to make gravy.
8. Serve with riced potatoes, hot noodles or rice. Yield: 6 servings.

62. HE-MAN HAM CASSEROLE

Ingredients

- 1/2 c. Chopped onion
- 1/2 c. Chopped green pepper
- 6 tbsp. Butter or margarine
- 6 tbsp. Flour
- 1/2 tsp. Pepper
- 1 1/2 c. Milk
- 1 c. Chicken broth
- 4 c. Cubed spam
- 1 (10 oz.) Pkg. Frozen beans
- 4 c. Hot seasoned mashed potatoes

- 1 egg, beaten
- 1 c. Shredded cheese

Preparation

1. Saute onion and green pepper in butter or margarine.
2. Add flour and pepper; stir until smooth.
3. Gradually stir in milk and broth.
4. Cook, stirring until thickened.
5. Combine with ham and beans in a 3-quart casserole. Combine mashed potatoes, egg and cheese.
6. Drop by spoonfuls onto mixture in casserole. Bake at 375° for 45 minutes or until bubbly. Makes 10 servings.

63. BAKED FISH WITH APRICOT SAUCE

Ingredients

- 1 1/2 lb. Fresh or frozen halibut or other lean fish steaks cut 1-inch thick
- 1/4 tsp. Garlic salt
- 1 (16 oz.) Can unpeeled apricot halves (in light syrup)
- 1 tbsp. Cornstarch
- 1 to 2 tsp. Curry powder
- 1 tsp. Soy sauce
- 1/8 tsp. Ground ginger
- 1/2 (8 oz.) Can sliced water chestnuts
- 1/4 c. Sliced green onions

Preparation

1. If using frozen fish, thaw. Cut into 6 equal portions and arrange in a 12 x 7 1/2 x 2-inch baking dish. Sprinkle fish with garlic salt; set aside.
2. Apricot Sauce: Drain apricots, reserving syrup. Cut apricot halves in two; set aside. Stir together reserved apricot syrup, cornstarch, curry powder, soy sauce and ginger in a small saucepan; cook and stir until thickened and bubbly. Remove from heat and stir in apricots, water chestnuts, and green onions. Spoon over fish.
3. Bake at 450°, uncovered, about 15 minutes or until fish flakes easily when tested with a fork. Makes 6 servings.

64. BAKED FISH WITH PAPAYA SALSA

Ingredients

- 1 1/2 to 2 lb. Thick, firm, fleshy fish fillets (sea bass, snapper, halibut, orange roughy)

- 1 c. Papaya salsa

Preparation

1. Preheat the oven to 350°.
2. Place the fish in a baking dish. Spread the salsa on top.
3. Cover with foil and bake for 10 minutes.
4. Remove the foil and continue to bake for 5 to 10 minutes longer or until the fish is tender and flaky.
5. Serve hot, garnished with cilantro sprigs.

65. CAJUN BLACKENED FISH

Ingredients

- 4 Tbsp. Margarine, melted
- 4 fish fillets
- 1/2 tsp. Onion powder
- 1/2 tsp. Garlic powder
- 1/2 tsp. White pepper
- 1/2 tsp. Black pepper
- 1/2 tsp. Cayenne pepper
- 1/8 tsp. Thyme
- 1/8 tsp. Sage
- 1/8 tsp. Oregano

Preparation

1. Spread melted margarine over fillets.
2. Combine all spices and mix well. Rub spices into fish.
3. Heat cast-iron skillet until very hot; watch carefully.
4. Cook fillets for about 3 minutes on each side, depending on thickness. (Caution: Cook outside or in a very well ventilated area.)

66. BEER FISH BATTER

Ingredients

- 1 1/2 c. Flour
- 1 c. Italian bread crumbs
- 3 eggs
- 3 tsp. Baking powder
- 1 tsp. Lemon pepper seasoning
- 1 can stale or flat beer

Preparation

1. Combine all ingredients.
2. If the batter is too thick, use water to thin.
3. Dip fish in batter and deep fry in hot oil.
4. Delicious with all vegetables: broccoli, peppers, parsley, mushrooms, onions, etc.

67. SHRIMP AND FISH CREOLE

Ingredients

- 1/2 lb. Shrimp, peeled
- 1 lb. Fish fillets, cut into small pieces
- 1 1/2 c. Chopped onion
- 2 cloves garlic, minced
- 1/2 c. Chopped green pepper
- 1 tbsp. Unsalted margarine
- 4 ripe tomatoes, peeled and coarsely chopped
- 2 tbsp. Chopped parsley
- 2 tsp. Paprika
- 1/2 tsp. Sugar
- 1/8 tsp. Cayenne pepper
- 1 bay leaf
- 1 tbsp. Cornstarch
- 1 tbsp. Water
- 1 c. Uncooked rice

Preparation

1. Sauté onions, green pepper, and garlic in margarine until tender.
2. Add tomatoes, parsley, paprika, sugar, cayenne, and bay leaf.
3. Cover and simmer 30 minutes. Add fish to sauce, then add shrimp.
4. Cook about 5 minutes, stirring occasionally until shrimp turns pink and fish flakes easily with fork. Blend together cornstarch and water.
5. Add to creole and cook, stirring until slightly thickened.
6. Meanwhile cook rice according to directions, omitting salt. Serve with Creole.

68. OVEN-FRIED FISH FILLETS

Ingredients

- 4 Tbsp. unsalted butter (1/2 stick), can substitute olive oil
- 2/3 C. crushed crackers (Ritz) OR cornflake crumbs
- 1/4 C. grated Parmesan cheese (about 1 oz.)

- 1/2 tsp. dried basil
- 1/2 tsp. dried oregano
- 1/4 tsp. garlic powder
- 1 lb. sole, scrod, perch or other mild-tasting fish fillets
- lemon wedges

Preparation

1. Preheat oven to 350 degrees. Melt the butter in a 9 x 13 pan in the oven.
2. While it melts, combine everything else except the fish, in a pie plate.
3. Dip the fish around in the melted butter, dip each piece of fish in the crumb mixture and return it to the baking pan.
4. Bake the fillets for 20 to 25 minutes, or until the fish flakes with a fork.
5. Serve with lemon wedges.

69. FISH STEW

Ingredients

- 1/2 lb. bacon
- 7 small white potatoes, peeled and sliced 1/4-inch thick
- 6 (3 oz.) fillets whitefish
- 3 large onions, peeled and thinly sliced
- salt and pepper to taste
- 2 (10.75 oz.) cans Manhattan-style clam chowder
- 1 (28 oz.) can crushed tomatoes
- 1 doz. eggs

Preparation

1. Line the bottom of a large pot with bacon.
2. Place a layer of potatoes over the bacon; then a layer of fish, in bite-size pieces; then a layer of onion slices, without separating the rings; and finally salt and pepper.
3. Repeat layers, not including bacon, and finish with a final potato layer.
4. Top with the chowder and crushed tomatoes. Can add 1 small can of tomato paste if you like a little more tomato flavor.
5. Pour in enough water so that all is covered.
6. Cover and simmer over medium heat until potatoes are tender, about 1 hour; bring heat back to a boil.
7. Crack eggs into the pot. Cook until eggs are done.
8. Serve with crackers and hot sauce.

70. LEMON BROILED FISH FILLETS

Ingredients

- 3 lb. Fish Fillets
- 6 Tbsp. Butter or Margarine
- 1 tsp. Salt
- 1/2 tsp. Pepper
- 1 Tbsp. Worcestershire Sauce
- 2 Tbsp. Lemon Juice
- Paprika
- 1/2 Cup White Wine

Preparation

1. Place fish in greased broiler pan.
2. Melt butter or margarine; mix with salt, pepper, Worcestershire sauce and lemon juice.
3. Brush fillets with this mixture. Sprinkle with paprika.
4. Broil 3 inches from source of heat for about 5 minutes or until golden brown.
5. Turn, brush again with sauce and sprinkle with paprika.
6. Broil 7 minutes longer until fish flakes easily when tested with a fork.

SIMPLE INGREDIENTS

FAST COOKING

71. AVOCADO EGG BOAT

Ingredients

- 1 medium Avocado
- Crumbled Bacon or Diced Ham
- 2 Whole Eggs
- Cheese
- Salt/Pepper

Preparation

1. Slice the avocado in half and remove the pit.

2. Use a spoon to scoop out 20% of the flesh.

3. Crack an egg into each half of the avocado.

4. Add salt and/or pepper to taste.

5. Sprinkle cheese, cooked bacon bits, or diced ham on top.

6. Place in the Air Fryer at 350F for 6-10 minutes.

72. HAM EGG AND CHEESE ROLLUPS

Ingredients

- 10 Slices of Ham
- 5 Scrambled Eggs
- 1 Tbsp. Butter
- Cheddar Cheese
- Baby Spinach
- Salt/Pepper

Preparation

1. In a large bowl, crack eggs. Whisk together with salt and pepper.
2. In a large nonstick skillet over medium heat, melt butter. Add eggs and scramble, stirring occasionally. Before eggs are fully cooked stir in cheddar cheese until melted, then stir in baby spinach until well combined.
3. On a cutting board, place two slices of ham. Top with a big spoonful of scrambled eggs and roll up. Repeat with the remaining ham and scrambled eggs.
4. Place roll-ups on top of the baking paper in air fryer and cook at 400F for 3-5 minutes or until ham is crispy.

73. CAULIFLOWER HASH BROWNS

Ingredients

- 1 Small Head Grated Cauliflower
- 1 Large Egg
- ¾ cup Shredded Cheese
- ¼ tsp Cayenne Pepper (optional)
- ¼ tsp Garlic Powder
- Salt/Pepper

Preparation

1. Grate entire head of cauliflower.
2. Microwave for 3 minutes and let cool. Place in cheesecloth and ring out all the excess water.
3. Place cauliflower in a bowl, add rest of ingredients and combine well.
4. Form into six square-shaped hash browns.
5. Place hash browns on top of the greased baking paper in air fryer and cook at 360F for 15-20 minutes.
6. Let cool for 10 minutes to allow hash browns to firm up.

74. SPINACH FETA QUICHE MUFFINS

Ingredients

- ½ Tbsp Butter
- ¼ Cup Onion
- 1 Clove Garlic
- 2 Ounces Cream Cheese
- 5 Ounces Frozen Spinach Thawed and Dry
- 3 Large Eggs
- 2 Ounces Feta Cheese Crumbles
- ½ Cup Mozzarella Cheese, Shredded
- 1 tsp Dijon Mustard
- Salt/Pepper
- 6 Slices Thin Deli Ham

Preparation

1. Spray 6 holes of an Air Fryer Muffin Pan with baking spray and line with 1 piece of ham per each muffin well.
2. In a medium frying pan, sauté the onions and garlic until translucent.
3. Add the cream cheese and stir until fully melted and ingredients are thoroughly mixed. Let simmer on low.
4. In a medium mixing bowl add the spinach, eggs, feta cheese, mozzarella cheese, salt and pepper and mix thoroughly.
5. Add the cream cheese mixture to the medium bowl and mix with a hand mixer until blended.
6. Divide the spinach feta quiche mixture evenly between the 6 muffin wells. About 1/3 cup per muffin well works perfectly.
7. Place Muffin Pan in Air Fryer and set to 360F. Cook for 22 minutes.

75. BREAKFAST CASSEROLE WITH FETA

Ingredients

- ½ Green Bell Pepper (cut into thin strips)
- ¼ tsp. Dried Oregano
- ½ Cup Cherry Tomatoes (sliced in half)
- ½ Cup Feta Cheese, Crumbled
- 5 Eggs
- Salt/Pepper

Preparation

1. Spray an Air Fryer Baking Dish with cooking spray.
2. Place green peppers into the baking dish, sprinkle with oregano and roast at 360F for 5-8 minutes.
3. Crack eggs into a bowl, sprinkle with salt and pepper and beat until well combined.
4. Once the green peppers are roasted, add the cherry tomatoes to the Air Fryer and roast for an additional 8-10 minutes.
5. Sprinkle feta cheese over the roasted peppers and tomatoes then pour the beaten eggs over.
6. Lightly stir to ensure the green peppers and tomatoes are evenly distributed in the eggs.
7. Cook for an additional 10-15 minutes, or until the top is lightly browned and eggs are set.
8. Serve hot with a dollop of sour cream if desired.

76. PUFF PANCAKE

Ingredients:

- 3 Eggs
- ½ Cup Sour Cream
- 2 Tbsp Splenda
- 1 tsp Baking Powder
- ¼ Cup Almond Flour
- 2 Tbsp Butter

Preparation

1. Add eggs, sour cream, Splenda, baking powder and almond flour into a blender and blend on high until all ingredients are thoroughly mixed.
2. Melt butter in an Air Fryer Baking Dish at 400F for 2-3 minutes or until the butter is bubbling.
3. Gently pour the batter over the hot butter and return to Air Fryer.
4. Bake for 15-17 minutes, until pancake is golden and puffed.
5. After baking, cut and serve warm.

77. KETO QUICHE

Ingredients

Almond flour crust

- ¾ Cup Almond Flour
- 2 Tbsp Grated Parmesan
- 1 Large Egg
- ¼ tsp Salt

Quiche one

- 1 Large Egg
- ½ Tbsp Heavy Whipping Cream
- 2 Slices Bacon (cooked)
- 4 Small Tomatoes
- ½ oz Mozzarella Cheese
- ¼ tsp Parsley
- Salt/Pepper

Quiche two

- 2 Large Eggs
- ½ oz Gorgonzola Cheese
- 1 oz Frozen Spinach
- ½ Tbsp Heavy Whipping Cream
- Salt/Pepper

Preparation

Almond flour crust

1. Combine the almond flour, parmesan, egg and salt and mix well until dough is formed.
2. Split the dough into two pieces and form into an Air Fryer Baking Pan.
3. Using a fork or knife make scored in the dough so the crust doesn't bubble in the Air Fryer.
4. Bake at 325F for 7 minutes. Allow cooling.

Quiche one

1. Layer the cooked bacon, mozzarella cheese, and tomatoes on the bottom of cooled crust.
2. In a bowl mix together the egg and heavy whipping cream and pour onto crust and fillings. Season with salt and pepper.
3. Bake at 350F for 15-20 minutes or until fully cooked through.

Quiche two

1. Layer cooked, thawed spinach and gorgonzola onto the cooled crust.

2. Combine the eggs and heavy whipping cream and pour over crust and fillings. Season with salt and pepper.
3. Bake at 350F for 15-20 minutes or until fully cooked through.

78. ZUCCHINI FRITTERS

Ingredients

- 1 Pound Zucchini
- 1 tsp Salt
- 2 Large Eggs
- 1 ½ Ounce Minced Onion
- 1 ½ tsp Lemon Pepper
- ½ tsp Baking Powder
- 1 Cup Almond Flour
- ½ Cup Grated Parmesan Cheese

Preparation

1. Grate zucchini into a bowl. Sprinkle with 1 tsp of salt. Gently mix to distribute salt and let sit for 5 minutes. Squeeze the zucchini out with your hands and place into a clean mixing bowl.
2. Add the eggs and onions to the zucchini and mix together.
3. In a small bowl, add the dry ingredients and stir together.
4. Combine the dry ingredients with the zucchini mixture.
5. Form into patties and place in Air Fryer.
6. Bake at 400F for 20 minutes or until fully cooked and crispy on the outside.

79. SHRIMP SCAMPI

Ingredients

- 4 tablespoons butter
- 1 tablespoon lemon juice
- 1 tablespoon minced garlic
- 2 teaspoons red pepper flakes
- 1 tablespoon chopped chives or 1 teaspoon dried chives
- 1 tablespoon minced basil leaves plus more for sprinkling or 1 teaspoon dried basil
- 2 tablespoons chicken stock (or white wine)
- 1 lb defrosted shrimp (21-25 count)

Preparation

1. Preheat Air Fryer to 330F. Place a 6 x 3 metal pan in it and allow the oven to start heating while you gather your ingredients.

2. Place the butter, garlic, and red pepper flakes into the hot 6-inch pan.
3. Allow it to cook for 2 minutes, stirring once, until the butter has melted. Do not skip this step. This is what infuses garlic into the butter, which is what makes it all taste so good.
4. Open the air fryer, add all ingredients to the pan in the order listed, stirring gently.
5. Allow shrimp to cook for 5 minutes, stirring once. At this point, the butter should be well-melted and liquid.
6. Mix very well, remove the 6-inch pan using oven mitts and let it rest for 1 minute on the counter.
7. Stir at the end of the minute. The shrimp should be well-cooked at this point.
8. Sprinkle with additional fresh basil leaves and enjoy.

80. BACON JALAPENO POPPERS

Ingredients

- 8 medium jalapenos
- 6 oz ground beef
- 8 slices bacon
- 2 oz Cream Cheese
- Salt/Pepper

Preparation

1. Place ground beef in a pan over medium heat and allow it to fully cook. Season with salt and pepper and set aside to cool.
2. Cut jalapenos in half lengthwise and remove the seeds.
3. Spread cream cheese inside each jalapeno half. Don't overfill with cream cheese or it will be hard to fit the ground beef in!
4. Add the ground beef on top of the cream cheese.
5. Cut each slice of bacon in half length-wise. Wrap the bacon around the jalapeno, being sure to trap all of the fillings in. We use 1/2 slice of bacon per popper.
6. Place poppers in Air Fryer at 400F for 10-15 minutes. Enjoy!

81. BROCCOLI AND CHEDDAR CHICKEN

Ingredients

- 2 Boneless, Skinless chicken breast cut in half
- 1 cup Shredded Cheddar Cheese
- 1 cup chopped broccoli
- Garlic Powder (to taste)
- Paprika (to taste)
- 1 tbsp Extra Virgin Olive Oil
- Salt/Pepper

Preparation

1. Cut slits in chicken.
2. Season chicken with olive oil, sea salt, pepper, garlic powder and paprika to taste.
3. Stuff chicken pockets with chopped broccoli and cheddar cheese (save some cheese to top chicken with later)
4. Place in an Air Fryer Baking Dish and cook at 400F for 10-15 minutes.
5. Sprinkle chicken with the remaining cheese.
6. Bake for an additional 3-5 minutes or until cheese is melted.

82. KETO CASHEW CHICKEN

Ingredients

- 3 raw chicken thighs boneless, skinless
- 2 tbsp canola oil(for cooking)
- 1/4 cup cashews
- 1/2 medium Green Bell Pepper
- 1/2 tsp ground ginger
- 1 tbsp rice wine vinegar
- 1 1/2 tbsp soy sauce
- 1/2 tbsp chili garlic sauce
- 1 tbsp minced garlic
- 1 tbsp Sesame Oil
- 1 tbsp Sesame Seeds
- 1 tbsp green onions
- 1/4 medium white onion
- Salt/Pepper

Preparation

1. Heat a pan over low heat and toast the cashews for 8 minutes or until they start to lightly brown and become fragrant. Remove and set aside.
2. Dice chicken thighs into 1-inch chunks. Cut onion and pepper into equally large chunks.
3. Place in Air Fryer at 400F for 5-10 minutes.
4. Once the chicken is fully cooked. Add the pepper, onions, garlic, chili garlic sauce and seasonings (ginger, salt, pepper). Allow cooking for an additional 2-3 minutes.
5. Add soy sauce, rice wine vinegar, and cashews and allow the liquid to reduce down until it is a sticky consistency, There should not be excess liquid in the pan upon completing cooking.
6. Serve in a bowl, top with sesame seeds and drizzle with sesame oil. Enjoy!

83. ROASTED PARMESAN BROCCOLI

Ingredients

- 1 large head of Broccoli sliced into 1-inch thick steaks
- 4 cloves garlic, thinly sliced
- 1 teaspoon salt and pepper
- Red pepper flakes
- 2 tablespoons parmesan
- Lemon zest from half a lemon
- 3-4 tablespoons olive oil

Preparation

1. Place sliced broccoli into Air Fryer.

2. Sprinkle with salt, pepper, red pepper flakes, and olive oil, toss gently.

3. Roast in Air Fryer for 10 minutes, add the sliced garlic to the broccoli and continue cooking for 6 more minutes.

4. Sprinkle with parmesan and bake for 2 more minutes.

5. Remove from the Air Fryer, dust with lemon zest and enjoy!

84. GARLIC LEMON AND PARMESAN ROASTED ZUCCHINI

Ingredients

- 1 1/2 lbs zucchini (about 4 - 5 small/medium zucchini)
- 2 Tbsp olive oil
- Zest of 1 small lemon (1 tsp)
- 2 cloves garlic, crushed through a garlic crusher or finely minced
- 3/4 cup finely shredded parmesan cheese
- Salt/Pepper

Preparation

1. Cut zucchini into thick wedges or halves (cut each zucchini in half then that half in half, so you have 4 wedges from each zucchini.
2. In a small bowl, stir together olive oil, lemon zest, and garlic.
3. Align zucchini in Air Fryer spacing them evenly apart.
4. Brush olive oil mixture over tops of zucchini.
5. Sprinkle tops with parmesan cheese and season lightly with salt and pepper.
6. Bake in Air Fryer at 375F for 8-10 minutes. Serve warm.

85. EASY CHICKEN FAJITAS

Ingredients

- 3-4 Boneless skinless chicken breasts
- 1-2 tsp Taco seasoning
- 2 Bell peppers in assorted colors, deseeded and thinly sliced
- 1 Red onion, peeled and thinly sliced
- 1-2 Tbsp Olive oil
- 1/2 Cup Shredded Cheddar or Mexican Blend Cheese

Preparation

1. Trim the chicken breasts then lay them in a single layer in Air Fryer.
2. Sprinkle the taco seasoning over the top of the chicken breast to taste.
3. Lay your thinly sliced onions and peppers on top of the chicken breast, spread out evenly over the top.
4. Drizzle the olive oil over the peppers and onions.
5. Sprinkle cheese over the top of the dish.
6. Bake in Air Fryer at 375F for 10-15 minutes or until chicken is cooked through and the juices run clear.

86. NO CRUST PIZZA BITES

Ingredients:

- Air Fryer Muffin Tin
- Thicker cut Canadian bacon
- Shredded Mozzarella cheese
- Pizza sauce
- Pizza toppings of choice

Preparation

1. Lightly grease Air Fryer muffin tin. Place 3 pieces of your thick cut Canadian bacon into each cup of your muffin tin. Press down into cups.
2. Drop 1 Tbsp. of sauce into each cup.
3. Add toppings and make sure they are decently full.
4. Top with a generous amount of Mozzarella cheese.
5. Place in Air Fryer and bake at 350F for 8-10 minutes or until the top is bubbly and golden brown.
6. Remove them from the pan using a fork to pop them out. There will be a little bit of juice to discard in the bottom of each cup.
7. Enjoy!

87. PHILLY CHEESE STEAK STUFFED PEPPERS

Ingredients:

- 8 ounces Thinly Sliced Roast Beef
- 8 slices provolone cheese
- 2 large green bell peppers
- 1 medium sweet onion
- 1 (6 ounces) package baby Bella mushrooms
- 2 tablespoons butter
- 2 tablespoons olive oil
- 1 tablespoon garlic, minced

Preparation

1. Slice peppers in half lengthwise, remove ribs and seeds.
2. Slice onions and mushrooms. Saute over medium heat with butter, olive oil, minced garlic and a little salt and pepper. Saute until onions and mushroom are nice and caramelized. About 15-20 minutes.
3. Slice roast beef into thin strips and add to the onion/mushroom mixture. Allow cooking 5-10 minutes.
4. Line the inside of each pepper with a slice of provolone cheese.
5. Fill each pepper with meat mixture until they are nearly overflowing.
6. Top each pepper with another slice of provolone cheese.
7. Bake in Air Fryer at 375F for 8-10 minutes or until the cheese on top is golden brown.

88. PIZZA STUFFED PORTOBELLO MUSHROOMS

Ingredients:

- 4 Portobello Mushrooms
- 4 tbsp Pizza Sauce
- 1 handful Mozzarella, grated (approx 1/2 cup)
- 1 handful Cheddar Cheese, grated (approx 1/2 cup)
- 2.6 oz (75g) Chorizo, sliced
- 1/2 Pepper/Capsicum (color of choice)
- 1/2 small Onion, finely diced
- 1 tsp Italian Herbs
- Salt & Black Pepper, to taste
- Olive Oil

Preparation

1. Remove the stalks and scrape out the gills with a teaspoon. Gently clean with a damp towel to remove any excess dirt.

2. Lightly coat with Oil and give a good seasoning of Salt and Pepper. Place face down in Air Fryer and bake at 400F for around 5 minutes or until they just begin to wilt and produce water.
3. Drain away/soak up the excess moisture.
4. Use the first layer of pizza sauce, then mozzarella and top with cheddar.
5. Evenly sprinkle the rest of your toppings and finish with a dusting of Italian Herbs. Pop back in the Air Fryer and bake for a few minutes until the cheese starts to crisp.
6. Enjoy!

89. BACON WRAPPED BRUSSELS SPROUTS - BALSAMIC MAYO DIP

Ingredients:

- 12 slices bacon
- 12 brussels sprouts, stems trimmed
- 12 toothpicks
- For the balsamic dip:
- 5 tablespoons mayonnaise
- 1 tablespoon balsamic vinegar

Preparation

1. Wrap a bacon slice around each brussels sprout, and secure with a toothpick. Place in a single layer on baking paper in Air Fryer.
2. Bake at 375F until the bacon is crispy and the brussels sprouts are very tender about 15-20 minutes.
1. Balsamic Dip:
2. Combine mayonnaise and balsamic vinegar together in a small bowl. Stir until smooth.
3. Serve the bacon wrapped brussels sprouts with the balsamic mayonnaise dip

90. BELL PEPPER NACHO BOATS

Ingredients:

- 1 pound ground beef
- 1 teaspoons chili powder
- 1 teaspoon cumin
- 1/2 teaspoon black pepper
- 1/4 teaspoon kosher or sea salt
- 3/4 cup salsa, no sugar added
- 1 cup grated cheddar cheese, reduced-fat
- 3 bell peppers

Preparation

1. Remove seeds, core, and membrane from bell peppers then slice each one into 6 vertical pieces where they dip down. Set sliced bell peppers aside.
2. Cook ground beef over medium-high heat, breaking up as it cooks. Cook through and drain fat.
3. Combine cooked ground beef with spices and salsa. Evenly distribute mixture into the bell pepper boats, top with cheese.
4. Place in Air Fryer on baking paper and bake at 375F for 8-10 minutes or until cheese is melted and peppers are hot.

91. CAPRESE GRILLED CHICKEN WITH BALSAMIC VINEGAR

Ingredients:

- 6 grilled boneless, skinless chicken breasts
- ¼ cup balsamic vinegar
- 1 tablespoon butter
- 6 slices mozzarella cheese
- 6 slices tomato
- 6 large basil leaves

Preparation

1. Prepare chicken in Air Fryer at 400F for 10-15 minutes or until cooked through and juices run clear.
2. As chicken is cooking, pour balsamic vinegar into saucepan or skillet and cook until reduced by half. Add in butter and stir with a flat whisk until completely combined. Set aside.
3. Top chicken with mozzarella cheese, basil leaf, and then tomato slice.
4. Drizzle with balsamic reduction and serve warm.

92. BUFFALO CHICKEN MEATBALLS

Ingredients:

- 1lb ground chicken
- 1 egg, beaten
- 2 sprigs of green onion, finely chopped
- 1 celery stalk, trimmed and finely diced
- 1 tablespoon almond or coconut flour
- 1 tablespoon mayonnaise
- 1 tsp onion powder
- 1 tsp garlic powder
- 1 tsp pink sea salt
- 1 tsp ground black pepper

- 1 cup of buffalo wing sauce

Preparation

1. Place baking paper in air fryer and spray with oil of choice.
2. In a large bowl, combine all ingredients, except the buffalo sauce. Mix well.
3. Use your hands to form 2″ balls, the mixture will be sticky.
4. Place meatballs in Air Fryer and bake at 350F for 15 minutes or until center has reached 160º.
5. Remove meatballs from the Air Fryer. Place in a skillet or pot over medium-low heat. Coat with buffalo sauce. Continue to cook just until sauce is warmed.

93. BACON WRAPPED AVOCADO

Ingredients:

- 2 Fresh and Firm Avocados
- Hickory Smoked Bacon
- Ground Cumin
- Chili Powder

Preparation

1. Simply slice firm avocados into wedges and peel off the skin.
2. Stretch thick bacon strips to elongate them. Cut them in half. Then wrap half a bacon strip around each avocado wedge and tuck the ends under the bottom.
3. Sprinkle the wedges with chili powder and cumin, and even a little salt. Don't go overboard on the salt, because bacon is already salty.
4. Bake the Bacon Wrapped Avocado slices in Air Fryer at 400F for 5-10 minutes or until the bacon is red and crispy.
5. Cool and enjoy!

94. CLASSIC BURGERS

Ingredients:

- 1 Tablespoon Worcestershire sauce
- ½ teaspoon garlic powder
- ½ teaspoon onion powder
- ½ teaspoon salt
- ½ teaspoon ground black pepper
- ½ teaspoon dried oregano
- 1 teaspoon dried parsley
- 1 pound 93/7 ground beef

Preparation

1. In a small bowl, mix together all the seasoning items.
2. Add the seasoning mix to the beef in a large bowl.
3. Mix well, but be careful not to overwork the meat as that leads to tough burgers.
4. Divide the beef mixture into 4, and shape the patties. With your thumb, put an indent in the center of each one to prevent the patties bunching up in the middle.
5. Place burgers in Air Fryer and spray tops with oil.
6. Cook for 10 minutes for medium (or longer to the desired degree of doneness). (no need to flip patties)
7. Serve hot on a bun with side dishes of your choice.

PIE RECIPE

95. BUMBLEBERRY PIE

A recipe for Bumbleberry Pie ran in 1990 with a jumble of berries (hence the name) and cherries in the filling. This time around, we used apple to balance the tart cranberries.

Ingredients

- 1 recipe 2-Pie Pastry
- 2 Gala or Fuji apples, peeled, cored and finely chopped
- 3 c. (12-oz.) cranberries
- 1 1/4 c. granulated sugar
- 1/2 tsp. ground cinnamon
- 1/4 tsp. ground ginger
- 1 c. (5-oz.) frozen blueberries

- 1 c. (4-oz.) frozen raspberries
- 1/4 c. cornstarch
- 1 tbsp. heavy cream
- 1 large egg yolk
- 3 tbsp. coarse sugar

Preparation

1. Preheat oven to 400 degrees F. On a floured surface, with a lightly floured rolling pin, roll on disk of 2-Pie Pastry recipe into a 12-inch circle. Transfer to 9-inch pie plate. Trim excess dough. Fold dough rim under; crimp as desired. Line crust with parchment paper; fill with pie weights or dried beans. Bake 15 minutes or until bottom is slightly dry. Remove parchment and weights. Bake 10 minutes or until golden; remove from oven. Reduce temperature to 375 degrees F.
2. Roll remaining disk into a 10-inch circle. With floured leaf-shaped cutters, cut out shapes from dough. Freeze cutouts on waxed-paper-lined plate or cookie sheet while making the filling.
3. Make filling: in 5-quart saucepot, combine apples, cranberries, sugar, cinnamon, ginger and pinch salt. Simmer on medium 10 to 15 minutes or until most cranberries burst, stirring occasionally. Remove from heat. To cranberry mixture, add blueberries, raspberries, and cornstarch. Place pie shell on the rimmed baking sheet. Add filling; spread evenly.
4. In small bowl whisk cream and egg yolk. Arrange cutouts all over the top of the pie. Brush shapes with cream mixture; sprinkle with coarse sugar. Bake 1 hour to 1 hour and 15 minutes or until crust is deep golden brown and filling is bubbly.

96. MAPLE GRANOLA PECAN PIE

Looking for a classic dessert with a twist? Try out this decadent pecan pie recipe.

Ingredients

- 1 c. regular oats
- .13 tsp. ground cinnamon
- 6 tbsp. melted butter
- 1 c. grade B maple syrup
- 2 tbsp. grade B maple syrup
- 1½ c. pecan halves and pieces
- ½ c. sweetened flaked coconut
- ½ package refrigerated piecrusts
- ½ c. firmly packed brown sugar
- 2 tsp. all-purpose flour
- ¼ tsp. salt
- 3 large eggs
- 2 tsp. vanilla extract

Preparation

1. Heat oven to 350 degrees F. In a small bowl, stir together oats, cinnamon, 2 tablespoons melted butter, and 2 tablespoons maple syrup until blended. Spread oat mixture on a lightly greased baking sheet. Bake 20 minutes or until oats begin to turn golden; remove from oven and stir in pecans and coconut. Bake 10 to 12 more minutes or until pecans and coconut are lightly toasted. Remove from oven and cool completely on a wire rack (about 15 minutes).
2. Fit refrigerated piecrust into a 9-inch pie plate according to package directions; fold edges under and crimp as desired.
3. Whisk together brown sugar and next 2 ingredients until blended. Add eggs, vanilla, remaining 4 tablespoons melted butter, and remaining 1 cup maple syrup, whisking until blended. Spoon pecan mixture into prepared piecrust; carefully pour maple syrup mixture over pecan mixture.
4. Bake at 350 degrees F on the lower oven rack for 35 to 40 minutes or until set. Remove from oven and cool completely on a wire rack (about 1 hour).

97. SWEET POTATO PIE WITH CORNMEAL CRUST

Ingredients

Pie crust

- 1¼ c. pastry flour
- ¼ c. fine cornmeal
- 1½ tsp. Kosher salt
- 1 tsp. sugar
- 1 stick unsalted butter
- 2 tbsp. unsalted butter
- ⅓ c. ice water

Filling

- 2¾ lb. sweet potatoes
- 4 tbsp. unsalted butter
- ⅓ c. granulated sugar
- 3 large eggs
- ⅓ c. unsweetened coconut milk
- 1¼ tsp. cinnamon
- ¾ tsp. ground ginger
- ¾ tsp. Kosher salt
- ¼ tsp. ground cloves
- 1 large egg
- Turbinado sugar
- Unsweetened whipped cream

Preparation

1. Make the Piecrust: In a food processor, pulse the pastry flour with the cornmeal, salt, and sugar. Add the butter and pulse until the mixture resembles coarse meal with some pea-size pieces of butter remaining. Sprinkle the water on top and pulse until the dough just starts to come together. Scrape the dough out onto a work surface, gather up the crumbs and pat the dough into a disk. Wrap in plastic and refrigerate until well chilled, about 1 hour.

2. On a lightly floured work surface, roll out the dough to a 13-inch round, a scant 1/4 inch thick. Ease the dough into a deep 9-inch glass pie plate. Trim the overhanging dough to 1 inch and fold it under itself. Crimp decoratively and chill the crust until firm, about 15 minutes.

3. Preheat the oven to 375 degrees F. Line the crust with parchment paper and fill with pie weights or dried beans. Bake in the lower third of the oven for about 20 minutes, until the crust is barely set. Remove the parchment and pie weights and bake for 20 minutes longer, until the crust is lightly browned; let cool. Increase the oven temperature to 400 degrees F.

4. Prepare the Filling: Poke the sweet potatoes all over with a fork and arrange them on a large, foil-lined baking sheet. Bake for about 1 hour, until tender. Let cool completely, then peel and coarsely mash. Measure out 3 cups of mashed sweet potatoes; reserve the rest for another use.

5. In a food processor, combine the butter with the granulated sugar and puree until smooth. Add the 3 cups of sweet potato and puree until very smooth. With the machine on, add the eggs 1 at a time until each is just incorporated. Add the coconut milk, cinnamon, ginger, salt and cloves and pulse until no streaks remain.

6. Scrape the filling into the cooled piecrust. Brush the rim with the egg wash and sprinkle turbinado sugar over the crust and filling. Bake for 45 to 50 minutes, until the filling, is just set but slightly jiggly in the center; cover the crust with strips of foil if it gets too dark. Let the pie cool completely, then cut into wedges and serve with unsweetened whipped cream.

98. DECADENT CHOCOLATE ESPRESSO PIE

Ingredients

- 1½ c. milk
- ⅓ c. cornstarch
- ¾ c. sugar
- ½ tsp. salt
- 1 tsp. instant espresso powder
- 3 large egg yolks
- 1 tsp. vanilla extract
- 1 bar semisweet chocolate
- 1 bar bittersweet chocolate
- 4 oz. milk chocolate
- 1 recipe baked Perfect Piecrust

Espresso Whipped Cream

- 1½ c. heavy whipping cream
- 2 tsp. heaving whipping cream
- 2 tsp. instant espresso powder
- 6 tbsp. powdered sugar
- Grated chocolate

Preparation

1. Whisk together 1 cup milk and cornstarch in a small mixing bowl until smooth.
2. In a 3 1/2-quart saucepan combine sugar, salt, and remaining 1/2 cup milk. Cook over low heat, stirring frequently until sugar is dissolved. Whisk in espresso powder and cornstarch mixture. Cook over medium heat until mixture thickens, about 5 to 7 minutes.
3. Whisk about 1/2 cup cornstarch mixture into egg yolks in a large mixing bowl. Whisk this back into espresso mixture in saucepan and cook over medium-low heat 5 minutes, or until mixture is thickened further.
4. Remove from heat and whisk in vanilla and chopped chocolate. Transfer to one prebaked and cooled Perfect Piecrust. Place plastic wrap directly onto filling (to prevent the film from forming). Let stand 1 hour; then refrigerate for 6 hours.
5. Microwave 2 teaspoons cream in a small microwave-safe bowl for 10 seconds. Stir in espresso powder. Place remaining cream in a chilled mixing bowl. Beat at medium-high speed until soft peaks form. Add powdered sugar, 1 tablespoon at a time, until medium-firm peaks form. Add espresso mixture, beating just until incorporated. Spread over chilled pie and top with grated chocolate.

99. BOURBON-PECAN PIE

Add a splash of bourbon to give your favorite pecan pie some extra punch.

Ingredients

Piecrust

- 2 c. all-purpose flour spooned and leveled, plus more for work surface
- 2 tbsp. sugar
- 1/2 tsp. kosher salt
- 3/4 c. (1 1/2 sticks) cold unsalted butter cut into cubes
- 3 tbsp. ice water

Pie Filling

- 1/2 c. (1 stick) unsalted butter, at room temperature
- 1 c. sugar
- 2 large eggs, lightly beaten
- 1/2 c. all-purpose flour spooned and leveled
- 2 tbsp. bourbon

- 1/8 tsp. Kosher salt
- 1 c. chopped pecans, plus more for serving
- 1 c. semisweet chocolate chips
- Whipped cream and chocolate shavings, for serving

Preparation

1. Make Piecrust: Preheat oven to 350°F. Pulse flour, sugar, and salt in a food processor until combined, 2 to 3 times. Add butter and pulse until mixture resembles coarse meal, 10 to 12 times. Add water, 1 tablespoon at a time, and pulse until large clumps form (add up to 2 additional tablespoons of water if needed). Gather dough into a ball, roll into a 3/4-inch-thick disk. Wrap in plastic wrap; chill 30 minutes.
2. On a floured work surface, roll dough to a 13-inch round. Transfer to a 9-inch pie plate; fold edges under to align with the rim of the plate; crimp. Freeze for 30 minutes. Line pie with parchment paper and fill with pie weights or dried beans. Bake until golden brown, 15 to 20 minutes. Remove pie weights and parchment and cool.
3. Make Pie Filling: Beat butter and sugar with an electric mixer on medium speed until combined, 1 to 2 minutes. Add eggs, flour, bourbon, and salt and beat to combine about 1 minute. Fold in pecans and chocolate chips. Transfer to parbaked piecrust, and bake until center is set, 30 to 35 minutes. Cool completely on a wire rack.
4. Serve topped with whipped cream, chopped pecans, and chocolate shavings.

100. PEAR CRUMB PIE

Ingredients

- 1 recipe unbaked Perfect Piecrust
- ¾ c. all-purpose flour
- ½ c. cold butter
- ¾ c. light brown sugar
- ½ c. old-fashioned oats
- ½ c. chopped toasted pecans
- ⅓ c. all-purpose flour
- 1 c. sugar
- 2 tsp. cinnamon
- 6 c. Bartlett pears
- ½ c. dried cranberries

Preparation

1. Roll out half the dough on a lightly floured sheet of parchment paper to 1/4-inch thickness (about a 12-inch circle). Fit into a 9-inch pie plate, crimping edges as desired. Refrigerate 30 minutes to 1 hour.
2. Preheat oven to 365 degrees F.

3. Cut butter into 3/4 cup flour, sugar, and cinnamon. Add pears and cranberries, stirring to coat. Pour into prepared crust. Top evenly with the pecan mixture. Place on a aluminum foil-lined rimmed baking sheet.
4. Bake at 365 degrees F for 70 minutes, or until bubbly and golden brown. Let cool completely on a wire rack.

101. DOUBLE-CRUST APPLE PIE

People with a passion for piecrust will appreciate this double-crust delight: Flaky layers of dough encase a sweet, sticky apple filling. Yum!

Ingredients

Pastry:

- 2 1/2 c. all-purpose flour
- 1/2 tsp. salt
- 10 tbsp. cold butter or margarine
- 6 tbsp. vegetable shortening
- 6 1/2 tbsp. ice water
- Apple Filling:
- 2/3 c. sugar
- 1/3 c. cornstarch
- 1/2 tsp. ground cinnamon
- 1/4 tsp. nutmeg
- 1/4 tsp. salt
- 3 1/2 lb. Granny Smith, Golden Delicious, and/or Braeburn apples
- 1 tbsp. fresh lemon juice
- 2 tbsp. butter or margarine
- 1 large egg white
- 1 tsp. sugar

Preparation

To prepare pastry

1. In food processor with knife blade attached, blend flour and salt. Add butter and shortening, and pulse until mixture resembles coarse crumbs. Sprinkle in ice water, 1 tablespoon at a time, pulsing after each addition, until large moist crumbs just begin to form.
2. Shape dough into 2 balls, 1 slightly larger. Flatten each into a disk; wrap each in plastic wrap and refrigerate 30 minutes or overnight. (If chilled overnight, let stand 30 minutes at room temperature before rolling.)
3. Meanwhile, preheat oven to 400 degrees. Place cookie sheet on rack in lower third of preheated oven to bake the pie on later.

To prepare apple filling

1. In a large bowl, combine sugar with cornstarch, cinnamon, nutmeg, and salt. Add apples and lemon juice, and toss to coat evenly.
2. On the lightly floured surface, with a floured rolling pin, roll larger disk of dough into 12-inch round. Ease dough into 9 1/2-inch deep-dish glass or ceramic pie plate. Gently press dough against bottom and up the side of plate without stretching. Trim dough edge, leaving 1-inch overhang; reserve trimmings. Spoon apple mixture into pie crust; dot with butter.
3. Roll remaining disk for top crust into 12-inch round. Center round over filling in bottom crust. Trim pastry edge, leaving 1-inch overhang; reserve trimmings. Fold overhang under; bring up over pie-plate rim and pinch to form a stand-up edge, then make a decorative edge. Brush crust with some egg white. Reroll trimmings. With a knife or cookie cutters, cut out an apple and/or leaf shapes; arrange on pie. Cut short slashes in the round to allow steam to escape during baking. Brush cutouts with egg white, then sprinkle crust, and cutouts with sugar.
4. Bake pie 1 hour 10 minutes or until apples are tender when pierced with knife through slits in crust. To prevent over-browning, cover pie loosely with a tent of foil after 40 minutes. Cool pie on wire rack 3 hours to serve warm. Or cool completely to serve later.

Printed in Great Britain
by Amazon